Tramp in Flames

Paul Farley is from Liverpool and n
Lancashire, where he is currently R<
Lancaster University. He has receive
Maugham Award and a Forward Prize for his first collection
of poems, and was the *Sunday Times* Young Writer of the
Year in 1999. His second collection, *The Ice Age*, won the
Whitbread Poetry Award in 2002.

Also by Paul Farley

The Boy from the Chemist is Here to See You

The Ice Age

Paul Farley   *Tramp in Flames*

PICADOR

First published 2006 by Picador
an imprint of Pan Macmillan Ltd
Pan Macmillan, 20 New Wharf Road, London N1 9RR
Basingstoke and Oxford
Associated companies throughout the world
www.panmacmillan.com

ISBN-13: 978-0-330-44007-3
ISBN-10: 0-330-44007-1

9 8 7 6 5 4 3 2 1

A CIP catalogue record for this book is available from
the British Library.

Printed and bound in Great Britain by
Mackays of Chatham plc, Chatham, Kent

i.m.

M.D.

Acknowledgements

Many thanks to: *Areté*, *Forward Book of Poetry 2006*, *Grand Street*, the *Guardian*, the *London Review of Books*, *The North*, *Poetry London*, the *Times Literary Supplement* and *The Yellow Nib*.

'An Ovaltine Tin in the Egg Collections at Tring' was provoked by the project *Wild Reckoning*, and was published in the anthology of that name (Gulbenkian, 2004). 'Civic' and 'The Big Hum' were each written for BBC Radio 3 and 4. 'A Pollen Calendar' was published in the catalogue that accompanied Rob Kessler's exhibition *Pollinate* (Wordsworth Trust, 2001) and 'A Great Stink' was written in response to Wordsworth's sonnet for '*Earth has not any thing to shew more fair*' (Wordsworth Trust, 2002).

P.F.

Contents

Tramp in Flames

The Front

It stood firm for a fortnight, a cloud coast
that marked the front. All along the west
it towered; a full pan from north to south
held it in view. We watched it from the beach
each day for signs of movement. It didn't budge.
I thought of a tidal wave, freeze-framed,
but didn't say. Somebody on the third night
described it as a parting of the Red Sea
and then I couldn't help but squint for seals
or fish caught in its watery updraft,
but saw nothing. At certain times of day
you would have sworn you looked upon a land mass
with terns and gannets nested in its darkness.
Once, it grew the grey lip of a carrier deck.
Sunsets came a few degrees early
and, backlit, it glowed like something molten,
the birds heading for home crossing its lid
like car adverts with the sound turned down.
A two-week high of learning to live with it,
of tuning into paperbacks and rock pools;
the way the thrill of snow-capped peaks in summer
will slowly thaw, become invisible
and be just *there*: so it was with the front.
On the last day we woke to rain as thick
as diesel slicking the windows, all the shadows
scattered, the light turned low. We were inside it.

Night Swim

No one's looking. Take off your clothes. Step in.
At the Ceremony of the Keys, the chief yeoman
is thinking, 'Fuck this for a game of soldiers.'
A car slows for a red light on a B-road
then speeds up into the oncoming nothing.
Inshore vessels move through pools of radar.
Cocky watchmen turn a blind eye everywhere.
No one's looking. Take off your clothes. Step in.

You're not withdrawing money or propping up
a friend in some foreshortened city square,
nor are you entering crawl spaces to feed
or moving, ghost-eyed, through the infra-red
in until-now-never-before-seen footage.
Those satellites are shooting stars; that hum
the sound of blood and both our nervous systems.
No one's looking. Take off your clothes. Step in.

No Life Room three-bar heater will come on
for a copse of easels to slightly readjust itself.
There is no mythical figure you can turn to,
or turn into. When you take the plunge you'll find
no glass-walled observation lounge; the night
is still, and so dark even Orion
has found himself outgunned by lesser stars.
So no one's looking. Take off those clothes. Step in.

The Lapse

When the cutting edge was a sleight, a trick of time,
we blinked our way through *Jason and the Argonauts*,
thrilled by the stop-motion universe,
its brazen Talos grinding like a Dock Road crane,
and the Hydra's teeth sown into studio soil
by Harryhausen, who got between the frames
like a man who comes in bone dry from a downpour
by stopping the world and snapping out a path
through glassy rods right up to his front door.

Something as simple as Edgerton's milk splash
stilled to an ivory coronet would do it,
keep us quiet for hours as we learned to understand
the howling gale we stood in. Chilled to the core
we gasped as Ursula Andress stepped from the flame
and the unseen British-Pathé make-up department
took down her face, applying gravity with a trowel.
And I'd have to say something was taken from us.

On the dead sheep's seconds-long journey to nothing
with maggots working like a ball of fire,
every now and then a long bone settled awkwardly
like a break in continuity. Like an afternoon
of finding out for ourselves what death smelt like.
Long afternoons. Lying on our backs watching clouds
with the slow Doppler of a plane being bowed across the sky.
Give us back the giant day. Give us back what's ours.

Ruin

I knew their names and shapes from books
before I saw real clouds.

The walk home from the optician
was full of wonders: birds

on wires, the vertical hold of rain,
a bus's destination,

as if I'd climbed out of a mist
onto a peak. I'd missed

a decade's middle distances
but I've been grateful since

as nothing now's too low or small
to honour: one dark brick

stares right back from its newbuild wall
to the ramparts of Uruk.

Liverpool Disappears for a Billionth of a Second

Shorter than the blink inside a blink
the National Grid will sometimes make, when you'll
turn to a room and say: *Was that just me?*

People sitting down for dinner don't feel
their chairs taken away / put back again
much faster than that trick with tablecloths.

A train entering the Olive Mount cutting
shudders, but not a single passenger
complains when it pulls in almost on time.

The birds feel it, though, and if you see
starlings in shoal, seagulls abandoning
cathedral ledges, or a mob of pigeons

lifting from a square as at gunfire,
be warned, it may be happening, but then
those sensitive to bat-squeak in the backs

of necks, who claim to hear the distant roar
of comets on the turn – these may well smile
at a world restored, in one piece; though each place

where mineral Liverpool goes wouldn't believe
what hit it: all that sandstone out to sea
or meshed into the quarters of Cologne.

I've felt it a few times when I've gone home,
if anything, more often now I'm old,
and the gaps between get shorter all the time.

The Newsagent

My clock has gone although the sun has yet to take the sky.
I thought I was the first to see the snow, but his old eyes
have marked it all before I catch him in his column of light:
a rolled up metal shutter-blind, a paper bale held tight

between his knees so he can bring his blade up through the twine,
and through his little sacrifice he frees the day's headlines:
its strikes and wars, the weather's big seize up, runs on the pound.
One final star still burns above my head without a sound

as I set off. The dark country I grew up in has gone.
Ten thousand unseen dawns will settle softly on this one.
But with the streets all hushed I take the papers on my round
into the gathering blue, wearing my luminous armband.

Brutalist

Try living in one. Hang washing out to dry
and break its clean lines with your duds and smalls.
Spray tribal names across its subway walls
and crack its flagstones so the weeds can try

their damnedest. That's the way. Fly-tip the lives
you led, out past its edge, on the back field;
sideboards and mangles made sense in the peeled
spud light of the old house but the knives

are out for them now. This cellarless, unatticked
place will shake the rentman off, will throw
open its arms and welcome the White Arrow
delivery fleet which brings the things on tick

from the slush piles of the seasonal catalogues.
The quilt boxes will take up residence
on the tops of white wardrobes, an ambulance
raise blinds, a whole geography of dogs

will make their presence felt. And once a year
on Le Corbusier's birthday, the sun will set
bang on the pre-ordained exact spot
and that is why we put that slab just there.

One by one the shopkeepers will shut
their doors for good. A newsagent will draw
the line at buttered steps. The final straw
will fill the fields beyond. Now live in it.

Pantoum of the Emergency

for my father in Malaya, 1949–51

My genome has found itself put to the sword:
the broad steeled parang of the tropical wood.
It filmed itself chopping the heads off big wheels
because nobody carried a camera.

The broad steeled parang of the tropical wood
hacked outwards though vines and deep into my dreams.
Because nobody carried a camera
it handed me on the black baton of a grip.

Hacked outwards through vines and deep into my dreams,
the damage goes on as a jumpy loop tape.
It handed me on the black baton of a grip
like an article of night, like a roll of bad film.

The damage goes on, as a jumpy loop tape,
like a record run down in the tropical night,
like an article of night, like a roll of bad film
that the jungle has found its way into and spoilt.

Like a record run down in the tropical night,
the needle lifts off and the big night still plays.
That the jungle has found its way into and spoilt
a more temperate night is beyond any doubt.

The needle lifts off and the big night still plays.
The shock of still being there comes like an axe-fall.
A more temperate night is beyond any doubt.
Lightning is pink on the bedroom wall.

The shock of still being there comes like an axe-fall.
It screens itself chopping the heads off big wheels.
Lightning is pink. On the bedroom wall
my genome has found itself put to the sword.

As the Crow Flies

Became an idea, a pure abstraction,
all black vector, a distance in air miles;
Watling Street on the wing, a one-track mind
hell bent against a white, wintering sky.

Civic

Somebody should write on the paranoia of pines
  I wonder, making my way down to the shore
    of the reservoir in the dark,
     ignoring the signs
     which warn of deep water;
   there's a spring underfoot made up
of a billion needles and cones that carpet the floor

and a criss-cross of roots that keep the earth in its place
  and so the water clear: I've read the reports
    of the city engineers, done my homework,
     and move through the woods
     warily, the canopy high above
  whispering, watching (though I'm about as far
from another human being as it's possible to get here,

from our cities where you're never more than a few feet
  from a rat; where cameras comb the streets
    all hours), looking over my shoulder
     and seeing myself
     like that footage of sasquatch;
   or the private eye in *Chinatown*, hired
in a drought to find out what's happened to all the water

when all at once it's before me, a great glassy sheet,
　dark trees and hillsides held upside down
　　in starlight: I've found Manchester
　　at source, in the blues
　　of a bathymetric map, in the clean
　and still repose before the nightmare of taps
and kettles. I scoop a cold handful up to my mouth

and taste the great nothing that comes before pipes
　pass on their trace of lead, before fonts
　　leech their peck of limestone,
　　before public baths
　　annihilate with chlorine.
　The mind, honeycombed with aqueducts,
laps on the walls of Nineveh or Imperial Rome

but this is where it begins, if we can describe
　water in such terms, with middles and ends.
　　I can hear the sluices – sound
　　carries at this hour –
　　and the start of the journey
　down, to the distant city, a steady roar
acting as water's own bar pilot, river guide, exit sign

and gravity holds open the door onto a man-made dark,
  culverts at first, and then the all-enclosing
    mysteries of pipe-work;
      a gentle incline
      and two-miles-per-hour
    average flow through the fell, blind
though sometimes proud when bridging a beck or ghyll

aloofly, sealed in concrete, on official council business.
  Two miles per hour; a hundred miles,
    so by my reckoning it'll take
      just over two days:
      if there was anybody else
    up here with me, I'd suggest 'Pooh sticks'
played out on a glacial, OS Pathfinder scale

or introduce those bright dyes I've seen used in the field
  in this very catchment area, turning streams
    a turbulent day-glo in a matter
      of stop-watched minutes;
      then catch a bus or train in my own time
    down to the city, and wait in the Albert Square
for the fountain to run orangeade, cream soda or dandelion-

and-burdock. You could walk: no Roman would have given
  a second thought to the hike, no Romantic neither.
   But this is water's pause for reflection.
    This is its downtime.
   Water seeking asylum
  lying low for a while, taking a chance
to gather its thoughts. Years ago, in the Liverpool Aquarium,

I read how the lungfish would dig into the parched
  riverbed, curl into a ball, secrete
   mucus, and generally do
    what it needed to
   to weather a spell between
  broad sheets of sudden rainfall that fell
weeks or months or years apart, wrapped up in itself;

though there was no word next to the tank on how water too
  needs to introspect, to find some high cistern
   or a road's camber after a storm
    that can hold a moon;
   those baths you see in fields
  plumbed into whitethorn, where the Green Man
might take his murky ablutions before going to ground

are favourites too. Wind from out of nowhere disturbs
  the signal. Some of these trees are mobile masts
    disguised as trees, I'm told, and this
      lake a reservoir
    disguised as a lake. It looks
  the part alright; in fact, has already starred
in films as body double to Como and Geneva

though it knows it's an offcomer, a baby in glacial terms,
  and nothing much has pooled and stuck. There's no
    host of golden daffodils, no
      Bluebird going down
    in black-and-white to rise
  again in colour, no Post Office Tower
leant like a dipstick to illustrate its unnatural fathoms,

just those rumours that seem to follow reservoirs around:
  a drowned village, church bells on rough nights,
    the souls who stood their ground
      calling from the depths,
    that kind of thing. Then a blackbird
  breaks cover, and its cries manage to sound
genuinely bereft for lost acres of thicket and undergrowth

and miles of hedgerow. A Water Board van snakes its way
  silently northwards up the A591
    along the opposite bank,
      and it's getting light
    so I step back into the trees
  not wanting to be seen by anyone.
In this poem disguised as a meditation on water

it's now as good a time as any to tell you, reader,
  how I've driven up to this spot in a hire car
    and stand at the water's edge
      drawn by a keen sense
    of civic duty: I plan to break
  the great stillness and surface of this lake-
cum-reservoir by peeing quietly into the supply

and no harm will come to anything or anyone. Consider
  this: no shoal will surface out of sync
    like driftwood; no citizens
      will draw a cold draught
    of LSD, or run a hot bath
  of nerve agent in two days' time. This act
is so small it will only really occur in the mind's eye

and those particles – smaller than rods and cones – that escape
  the filters and treatment plant won't register
   in any sense. And so my ripples
     head for God-knows-where
    as light strengthens by increment
   and a tree falls in the woods and no one hears,
though I can't swear to any of this: I wasn't here.

Somebody else packed up in a hurry, walked back
  up a slope, bastard tricky with roots, came to
    the quiet road in the green shade
      that leads round the lake;
     passed a city's coat of arms
    and some Latin he couldn't read, looked out
from a wall across a body of water at chest height

and gasped at the thought of the pressure, the pounds-per-brick,
  and felt alone up there then, and wanted to drive
    far away from those high offices,
      from the danger signs
     where water stands in the hills
    with the eyes, from the man-made distances
that have haunted his ears; from the paranoia of pines.

A Great Stink

. . . but in fifty years the Commons will complain
they can't sit in this river's smell and soak
their curtains in chloride of lime to take
the edge off what they'll liken to a drain.
'King Cholera' will rise from *Punch* and walk
abroad with a peg on his nose. No poetry
will get written, save those olfactory
pieces papers commission: *This smell's a baulk*
to anything the eye can register
and crossing here is hazardous to health
at dawn, when all the night soil of Westminster
meets with a flood tide. Citizens of wealth,
flee for the summer while the city festers
and strike out for the coast like merde *yourselves.*

Duel

Split pistols on a woodchip wall a decade,
faked alloys, brandished, facing one another
above a brick fireplace (another bullshitter –

ersatz and cold). These two bisected bastards
were only half there, but they stared me down.
The horse brasses and Spanish fans were harmless

but guns form in the womb. If my dad was out,
bored, I'd take up arms and clasp each half
together, then I'd pick a photograph

along the mantelpiece, and draw a bead
between the eyes of some ancestral second;
or (this was harder) turn the pistol on

myself. I'd hold its shape along the midline
by sucking the muzzle – it tasted of television –
and use my thumbs to blow my fucking brains out.

Automatic Doors

When I see some kids springing the gallery doors
I lament the great revolvers. As we enter
a new era of doors, I can remember
the thrill involved, the stately, dumb inertia

at first, before they'd give, a slow surrender
to four heaving kids, storing our power,
a glass and darkwood turbine; how whatever
effort we put in, the doors would answer

as they gathered speed, until only a shoulder
nudge was needed (and though no passengers
were carried, now and then I'd grab the bar
and dangle in my quadrant). We'd spin for hours

or so it seemed: we were time travellers
fast-forwarding ourselves into the future
before we were thrown out, into an era
of never even having to lift a finger.

Tramp in Flames

Some similes act like heat shields for re-entry
to reality: a tramp in flames on the floor.
We can say *Flame on!* to invoke the Human Torch
from the Fantastic Four. We can switch to art
and imagine Dali at this latitude
doing CCTV surrealism.
We could compare him to a protest monk
sat up the way he is. We could force the lock
of memory: at the crematorium
my uncle said the burning bodies rose
like Draculas from their boxes.

                                  But his layers
burn brightly, and the salts locked in his hems
give off the colours of a Roman candle,
and the smell is like a foot-and-mouth pyre
in the middle of the city he was born in,
and the bin bags melt and fuse him to the pavement
and a pool forms like the way he wet himself
sat on the school floor forty years before,
and then the hand goes up. *The hand goes up*.

Johnny Thunders Said

You can't put your arms around a memory.
The skin you scuffed climbing the black railings
of school, the fingertips that learned to grip
the pen, the lips that took that first kiss
are gone, my friend. Nothing has stayed the same.
The brain? A stockpot full of fats and proteins
topped up over a fire stoked and tended
a few decades. Only the bones endure,
stilt-walking through a warm blizzard of flesh,
making sure the whole thing hangs together,
our lifetimes clinging on as snow will lag
bare branches, magnifying them mindlessly.
Dear heart, you've put a brave face on it, but know
exactly where the hugs and handshakes go.

Requiem for a Friend

after Rainer Maria Rilke

My dead are doing fine and are at home
wandering off the street into a night class
or half-lit drinking school among their own,
glad to be out of it. But since you've gone
on ahead – forgive the spatial shorthand,
it's all that works in this world – I've been troubled
by little things: a polystyrene cup
edging across a table on the train
like contact at a séance; a squirrel who stops
and eyes me sadly through the kitchen window;
opposites of portents, things that have me stand
to damp a past soon as I feel it build.

   This is a worry. I never had you down
as someone who'd stray back, being the sort
on even terms with the dead, and never one
for doing things by half; lighting your breath
on overproof rum, and other party tricks
for sure, but mostly your approach to the art
convinced me that you'd fit right in 'out there';
so why is it when a radiator knocks
I think of you as frightened? They say Death
requires that those left behind secure
their minds, and can arrange a late-night visit
for an audience of one; others go looking
and tune in to a mighty passing trade;
and the medium of the page is close to hand,
but until the words choose me I'm left with things

going bump: and these all say you want back in.
The opposite – again – of birds that board
a tube carriage for crumbs, but just as afraid
on the journey between stops. Is this what friends
are for: to say the door is always open?
Heart on the latch, I lie awake and listen.
Classic haunts demand some bricks and mortar
and yours are London stock. Their soot-caked yellow
constructs a meeting place on every corner
and draughty rooms you read your poems in,
though the herringbone tweed you wore each winter
disturbs the steady signal of the pointing
so sightings have been abundant – across streets
I've watched you blur into shopfronts and windows –
and now even the tolling of a skip
being filled, or a door slam in the downstairs flat
are noises off, a loud prompt from the wings;
they run a thumbnail down the cellophane
sleep wraps me in, and strip it. So. What's up?

Instead of begging at the station mouth
are you trying to press the all-zones travel pass
of night into my palm? Should I explore
a city just a few shades out of whack
from this, built in its shadows of slant rain?

Then I'll enter into it: I'll climb its stairwells,
its steps that won't add up; I'll stand for hours
and learn to make myself invisible

as its buskers do; I'll walk from north to south
approaching all its Big Issue vendors
on their blind sides; I'll mark the surfaces
where women straighten hair and fix their lipstick,
sift through an Oxfam shop's doorway moraine;
paused on the threshold of a tattoo parlour
I'll be in two minds – neither one thing nor the other –
and down one street I'll find a taxidermist
who deals in urban fauna, mesmerised
by a fox's backward glance, a pigeon's arabesque,
a feral cat's gelled hackles. This city casts
strange shadows and is full of trapped light, closed
out back in meat safes, stockrooms, nurseries,
the curtained blood glow of insomniacs,
of penlights shone into a captive's mouth,
of hands placed over torches deep inside
a cave system, of faces turned to masks.
I'll leave before that moment loved by guides
the world under: *Now turn your torches off.*

   If there was one thing you knew inside out
it was illusionism, the ticket hall
of mirrors, and we were taken for a ride
as willing passengers along a strong-line
not found on Beck's map or The Great Bear,
barely skimming the surface, then rattling down
to coalmine depths. Dropping your knife or fork
you'd frown skywards as if the object fell

from some great height. It had: Washington Square
in the rain, where you'd watched Robert Lowell's quart
of liquor shatter when his brown bag broke
and he looked up to heaven or low cloud.
To prove there were a downside to each joke
the ground gives way if someone tries this now.

It seems there was a world before I knew you,
a world I was at large in, but back then
its plate glass and its mirrors just confused
or startled me with angry slaps of sun.
You showed me how to move about this stage,
so why now are you banging into things
and throwing your weight around? Did you leave clues
strewn like flowers up to your final afternoon?
Should I have seen or read an evil omen,
in a house whose front and back doors had blown open,
an unexpected bar of small-hours birdsong,
or breaking news of flash floods through a village?

Slip into the light. See if I'm afraid
to look you in the face. When the dead return
they've every right to step out from the shadows
and harden once more in our field of vision.

Slip into an element more visible
as someone moving through the dark will trip
a lamp sensor outside and flood the garden
with halogen, a false dawn for the rose
and December moth, which comes to light – but real

enough for a few seconds – so a shade
can stand before us plain as day, even though
we know its sun lies deep in the horizon.

It takes a while to grasp but I think I know
the worst: sometimes I have you waking up
inside a funhouse room, the ceiling trying
to rain above the mosh-pit of your bed,
and as the paper peels in long sad scrolls,
you inch your way as firemen feel ahead
using their knuckles down a smoke-filled hall
(because a hand that feels its way palmwards,
if shocked, can trip and grab live wiring),
finding a snow globe boiled dry, a mirror
blackened and cracked, the brickwork kiln-hot,
and sometimes pass, eyes streaming, into chambers
of utter loss, carbon-encrusted dark
like houses where the roof has gone, from childhood,
abandoned to what wind blows through. In short
you find a place of pure aphelion.
You let the night get in; invited it.
Just shadow by shadow at first, as bar room smoke
entered the exoskeleton of your coat
and found a home there with the poisonous looks
and sly remarks absorbed, the ones you never
reflected back, with interest. Lifting it
onto its peg, I have you frisk its warmth

and deep inside its bottomless pockets
winkle what feel like seeds along its hems.
Gallstones, fulgurites – but still you pick the fluff
from them like ancient mints and are surprised,
alone there at the end of some lost night,
to find some trace of sweetness has survived.
Inside your senses you were sweet enough.

Time to lament. Your cometary blood
lost track; the circuit broke; how could it know
its point-of-no-return was being crossed?
A stanza-break can stand between two seasons
but blood is curious and your blood rushed
amazed into a room it never knew,
escaping from its greater circulation.
This party was worth crashing. If you could
you'd always stuff your pockets, weigh up ashtrays,
and stretch the hospitality to its limits;
your blood was no different. Ill-bred, it flung
itself through halls of everything you'd thought,
a slow stain on a scan but from the ground
perfect cathedrals, chambers of errors.
Trouble was, such sightseeing leads down slipways
that take you into Time, and Time is long,
and Time runs down, and Time slams all the doors,
and Time is like a medium's lapse in recall . . .

Your leaving as the days began to shorten
has left me wondering if the hours you spent
back here sent leader shoots, mycelial
pathways into your futures, as we all
could go so many ways each given moment.
And if one message came back through the drowned
Bronx subways, or the scorched earth of North London,
meaning you knew, or knew as threads in soil
weave through the dark, build instinct in the hope
of being heard before the nights draw in.

(Nothing. No spinal shiver. No failing light
the moment you sat bolt upright in bed
and called out, isolated as a sea stack.
No boom of blood like waves crashing inside
a cellar. All the skilled, frantic attentions
around you didn't register. As wars
and weather systems do their worst, as seabirds
must wheel now at the world's edge, others sleep.
Until bad news comes falling from the heights
of column inch or midnight call, we walk
the same old world, even as each distant landslide
re-writes the coves and inlets of its shores.)

And so you died and were put out to sea
from a neuro ward early on a Thursday evening,
lights coming on as nurses snipped you free
of oxygen mask, wires, indwelling needles,
the night schools silent for summer re-opening,

their door bolts scraping through old ruts and puddles.

Once there'd have been a right to-do: coloraturas
on wax cylinders; daguerreotypes; death masks,
where now we all observe small silences
or fail to rise to feature desks' requests.
The high styles have all gone or been disowned.
Could this be why you've come back: to flesh out
the bone-clack of lament? Can you hear me?
I'd like to spray my voice out like a mist net
over the slivers of your death, and rag
my range – from shout to whisper – down to tatters
so all my words would have to go round bare-arsed
and shivering in the snarls of that torn voice.
Lament never being enough, I'll point the finger:
no one person withdrew you from your tasks
(and anyway, he's everywhere and nowhere)
but I accuse him: you know who you are.

Whenever, walking through the day, I'm mugged
by some transporting detail – say the sound
of rain feeding a puddle on the platform
from one cracked pane a hundred feet above me –
then I don't want to know. I'd sooner warm
to a galaxy of pigeon shit than dwell
on ideas of angels crying in anger.

All this suffering has lasted far too long,
we can't bear it: it's grown too big to handle,
a generator of mechanical love

which runs itself and barks up trade and makes
a profit out of showing us our loss.
Who really has a right to their possessions?
And how can any of us hold onto things
that cannot hold their own selves; who can catch
themselves whole, as they glance past their reflections?
That childhood trick is gone. No more than divers
can grasp the light that leads them onto wrecks,
nor any of the bright groupers or wrasse
survive the sudden bends back to the surface,
the tonnes of air; so we can't call back one
who, unaware of us now, moves along
a narrow beam of single thought and faith
that keeps the great night out, that sees him safest:
unless we have a calling to do wrong.

Because this is wrong, if anything is wrong:
not to unlock the freedom of a love
with all the inner freedom we can summon.
In love, you only need respect one truth:
let go. Any infant's finger-grip will prove
how holding on comes easy. We must unlearn it.

You're not still here? Still hiding in some corner?
Nothing you didn't know already, I learned it
mostly from you. You seemed to pass through days
wide open, opposite to shade. First light
on Green Lanes. Love is walking home alone

and art is one long runner, an escape
in nothing like real time: both courses meet
and this is where you live, an attitude
that will outlast the big dune shifts, the minor
aftershocks. You'd already withdrawn
beyond us all, slipped out the back, split early
before the slow dance and the house lights up,
into the ashen dawn of your sixth decade,
leaving the customary great unfinished
poem: the one that has to stay unfinished.
    If you are still here, moving through the darkness,
if my voice has found a sympathetic resonance
and solid things are stirred on shallow sound waves,
then hear me out, and help me out. It's easy
to slip and lose our balance, and it's *back
to your post* and *look busy* and *here's your desk*.
One day, just sat there staring at my hands,
a pulsing in their vein-work broke a spell
just for a dreamlike moment. It happens: blood
reminding blood. And anyone who heaves
their own will know, the law of gravity
can pull it back to weight and worthlessness.
Between our little lives and the great work
there is bad blood, pent up, an ancient feud.
You'll understand if anybody will.
    But don't come back. If you can stand it, stay

dead with the dead. The dead have their own tasks.
But help me, in your own time, in your own way,
as far-off things can help us: deep within.

Filler

This doodle darkening my delegate pack
   on the sixth day of a seven-day conference
is keeping me from screaming. I have this knack
   for honeycombing out the present. Once
I didn't, and the world would turn to filler.
     Not hardnosed economics, like the soldier
     being sent up to the front, or why our butcher
saw fit to scoop sawdust into his mince.

Neither makeweight nor object from the past
   sticking it out from surplus-to-requirements
to value; time sanctifying waste.
   Not superstitious acres farmers grant
     to their crop devil, or a brewer's angels' share.
For me, none of this was strictly filler.
     I saw the use in test-cards and screen-savers.
     Even *Farley, get in goal!* bore fruitful stints.

But never listening to Horace, nor my mother,
eternity turned everything to filler,
our landscapes ground in time to a fine powder,
the bones of Stone Age man, readers and writers,
   the great iron ships, the balance sheets, the sales spikes,
     the last plant standing ancient history,
a sun like blood. Next thing, I'm waving *Goodbye!*
to the hydrogen atom as the seas boil dry,

which is no way to live. So I take shelter
in the moment's coral, careful not to look
into the whirlpool of the conference clock.

Philistines

They enter here and leave here through the big doors
    and pass by, unnoticed, though if you watch
any city street your eyes can learn to lock
    onto them. Follow the money. Find your big coat
and get outside: all this looking out the window
    puts daylight between things. Keen as a razor
you see them now: fuzzy-edged, in need of razors
    or loaded down with bags, slamming the doors
of taxis; stood in pairs at shop windows
    absorbed in a new season, keeping watch
from bus shelters, nodding to iPods, coats
    stinking with rain. A mechanism locks
them outside Wittgenstein and Kant and Locke,
    outside *The Rights of Man* or Occam's Razor;
prevents them slipping Arnold in their coats
    or hearing what's beyond the Frostian door;
admiring *Las Meninas* or *The Night Watch*,
    or writing sestinas in Word for Windows.
Do they see a world we miss, squeegeeing our windows
    or cutting keys to fit our abstract locks?
When she tweezers up the mainspring of a watch
    does it feel like giving birth? When he strops razors
or applies gloss to a freshly sanded door,
    what riptides flood the arm with every stroke and coat?
Their low puns and their proverbs used to coat
    your tongue, but now you pity them at windows
ghostly in plasma light, smoking in door-

ways, scraping back long bolts, checking locks
half cut on supermarket shiraz or
    sauvignon blanc before turning in. They watch
the clock. Sometimes a boss will tap his watch
    and shake his head, slowly. Poor bastards. Coats
never visit theatre cloakrooms; angry razor-
    burn blooms in call centres without windows
where Post-Its stick like shit to shoes. They'd lock
    horns with the likes of you. Get back indoors
where razors glide, where windows hiss tight shut,
    where watches flow, where coats dream on their pegs
and doors lock with a satisfying *click*.

Mongrel

When she dreams, kicking on the kitchen floor
or whining softly to herself in the shade,
it could be she's an Airedale again
aloof with strangers at a gate in Bradford;
a Border terrier, worrying no-man's-lands
between counties; ragging a rat from her jaws,
the legend of some overrun mill town;
or a toy breed, even, scooped into gloved hands.
Then she bares her teeth, as if to say it goes
much further back than that, and checks the start
of something cute on my part, who can't know
what pulls the leashes of her sinews taut,
nor understand the huge thing that pursues
her through the dark and deep world outside ours.

Whitebeam

The sixty-miles-per-hour plants, the growth
that lines the summer corridors of sight
along our major roads, the overlooked
backdrop to 'Preston, 37 miles'.
Speed-camera foliage; the white flowers
of Mays and Junes, the scarlet fruits of autumn
lay wasted in the getting from A to B.
Hymn to forward-thinking planting schemes,
though some seem in two minds: the greenwood leaves
are white-furred, have a downy underside
as if the heartwood knew in its heart of hearts
the days among beech and oak would lead to these
single file times, these hard postings,
and civilised itself with handkerchiefs.

Winter Games

Very comfortable in that skeleton
the commentator says during one run.

This is sport stripped down to the bare bones,
as democratic as a childhood tea tray,

familiar as a frost fair out of Breughel.
Almost faster than the camera's pan.

Thousandths of a second separate
world-record holders from the also-rans.

The women achieve the same speeds as the men,
very comfortable in their skeletons.

An Ovaltine Tin in the Egg Collections at Tring

If, at the end of the day as they say, these eggs
tell a story set in negative space, then it's right
the tin I caught sight of stacked in a corner
should have its say, a battered by-product
brought in after a spring-clean or a clear-out;
I could play it over my knee, bash out a tune,
but prefer to let this one speak for itself,
emptied twice over, if you see what I mean,

shiny inside, metallic as the moon,
the outside meant for a world I don't understand
just as a blackbird's egg seems out of place
laid out on cotton wool, removed from leaf shadow
or nettle bed. Caskets for collections
of garden birds, I say speak for yourselves
and there's just a huge silence of course, although
the brand names call out, as they were designed to:

Craven A, Huntley & Palmers, Oxo,
Crawford's, Jacob's, Peak Frean's Assorted Creams,
Selesta Fondants, Ogden's, Ovaltine . . .
Some sing on while others ring hollow,
a half-remembered jingle from the undergrowth
that turns this tin into a kind of music box,
and when I push and seal the lid back on
there's a silence twice over, if you see what I mean.

The Heron

One of the most begrudging avian take-offs
is the heron's *fucking hell, all right, all right,*
I'll go the garage for your flaming fags
cranky departure, though once they're up
their flight can be extravagant. I watched
one big spender climb the thermal staircase,
a calorific waterspout of frogs
and sticklebacks, the undercarriage down
and trailing. Seen from antiquity
you gain the Icarus thing; seen from my childhood
that cursing man sets out for Superkings,
though the heron cares for neither as it struggles
into its wings then soars sunwards and throws
its huge overcoat across the earth.

The Big Hum

I'm on the edge of a reed bed, just before dawn,
a slight breeze and a clear sky growing light.
That *chirruc* is a reed warbler close by.
As the birds grow active, I become stock-still

and part of the landscape, which lends my voice
that furtive veritas of cigarettes
across no-man's-land, Attenborough with the apes;
an intimacy with the baffled mic

in my small-hours stakeout. Miles of tape
wind through the twilight, getting it all down.
You can hear a nightjar crooning in the distance.
That booming bittern needs no introduction.

A black-headed gull going over seems to scold
that my half of the bed is growing cold,
and you can close your eyes and open up
a great space, stitched by wrens and plumbed by larks.

Installed in ditch or hedge, I've learned to keep
the manmade at arm's length from an early age
out on the city's edge, my own unbroken voice
a running commentary on what it heard.

But I don't romanticise the birds, like poets.
Their songs are strictly territorial,
perfumed and glandular, bitter as gall,
a media spend on advertising, or

their KEEP OUT signs, their re-election campaigns
sung to rivals up and down the food chain,
their contact calls, instant graffiti, bursts
declaring they've survived a night of frost.

My natural enemies are wind and rain,
a turbine coming over the earth's curve
that nobody can see but I can hear.
I keep away from roads and rush hours.

Still, even on mornings when I've found
a niche so isolate from rumble, hiss
or cattle; a spot that I could call my own
to the extent that you could score a radius

and say with some degree of certainty
I am the loneliest person in these Isles,
even beyond the high posts of rain gauges
and transmitter masts, I've heard this sound:

I call it The Big Hum. I've heard it on
the stillest, most remote of nights. It seems
as if all this attentiveness to background
has teased me to a greater tuning in

and I can hear the room tone of the world
like an approaching storm. I blamed the blood
spiralling through my ears at first, but there
it was, picked up on tape. Others have tried

explaining it in terms of The Big Bang,
a vestige of which vibrates in the silence
of five-bar gates and stones. Then there are those
who've understood eternal Sanskrit noise

to be the cause. I'm not having any of this.
From the damp and dead legs of the first position
of level meter and boom microphone,
I've heard the gain cranked up over the years.

And so I've made a tape for a winter evening
at home, when the only trace of birdsong
is a blackbird guttering down under a street-lamp.
A tape in which I count the species in

one by one into the studio's ark
before The Big Hum drowns them out. It starts
with a ring ouzel calling from the crags
of the Clwyd Hills in nineteen-eighty-six,

and then a heron from north Lancashire
on an overcast morning in ninety-four
leads deep into the Fens and nightingales
of seventy-seven, then passages of dippers

sung counterpoint to the exact babble
of the Cumbrian streambeds they lived beside,
and ravens *honking* high above the fells
of three decades ago, and all the warblers

of Oxfordshire and Gloucestershire I hardly knew;
I splice and overdub, and take it right
out to the edges' kittiwakes and gannets
where the sea drinks up the analogue signal

and have to shout over everything happening at once,
the whole island a bird colony, the song
and calls of forty springs to see me through
the dark winter ahead. Until I press STOP.

A Pollen Calendar

Wordsworth wouldn't know
these syllabic offcomers:
Japan still tight closed.

*

Watching the birds feast
on coconut, seed and fat
while we observe Lent.

*

A junk-mail promise
to help our home finances
blossom: straight in bin.

*

Hear the Manx mail plane?
The Doppler of half-past-one
crop-dusting our dreams.

*

Million, billi-
on, trillion, quadrilli-
on: the pollen count.

*

Summer's circulars:
cornflower, forget-me-not
on a hiker's boot.

*

'Carefully remove
any dust from your Nikon's
lens with some dry lint.'

*

A walk round the lake
that night of the Perseids'
split-second annuals.

*

Geese leaving in fives
and sevens: sales of anti-
histamines falling.

*

Resident poet
given free board to ponder
his propaganda.

*

Two business cards
from an Ambleside plumber
on our mat: first frost.

❋

Took this saijiki
up Silver How in the snow
with a flask of tea.

'A Shepherd's Guide to Wool and Earmarks'

Did Moses Mossop sit above Bowmanstead
with a book in early nineteenth-century rain?
He could have done: a drop has smudged his entry
in this knackered *Shepherd's Guide*, where Herdwicks graze

identically on every recto page
but for a second running through the press
that added the earmarks, and so identified
each flock to owner, and kept things up-to-date;

and sheltering by a sheepfold's leeward wall
he might have studied this on afternoons
of deepening lows, with fine drizzle broadcast
across each chapter – Seascale to Subberthwaite –

admiring these perfect, printed sheep,
his mind breeding a May of perfect lambs;
or thumbed its pages quickly so the ears
flickered to life and leapt like inky flames,

and with such animations passed his hours
as mine do, marooned in this dark hostel
with its puzzles and whodunits, all the paths
taped off and bleached, the scene of some huge crime.

A God

A god who checks you've turned the oven off
in some unnumbered radio galaxy
never sleeps or swerves from His one duty.
You never know: in the middle of the night
you could be up putting a pizza in,
and what does He care? It's the Middle Ages

where He lives. Watching over your stove
beats anything closer to hand: in two places
at once, He'd rather listen to the ticks
of the oven preheating than sit through jousts
or another spit roast. He enjoys the rings
glowing concentrically in your dark kitchen;

planetary, He thinks. Music of the spheres.
Hell, in his pianoless world, what He'd give
to stand before it like an instrument
and set its greasy dials for the hearts of suns,
careful not to raise the number of the beast
on its console – that would be a mistake –

but play all night bathed in its infra-reds;
electric music (the god of hearth
is banging from His sealed-up chimney breast),
ammonia, wire wool, black residue
on the brain pan, the upright honky-tonk
of metals cooling down when morning comes.

The Scarecrow Wears a Wire

The scarecrow wears a wire in the top field.
At sundown, the audiophilic farmer
who bugged his pasture unpicks the concealed
mics from its lapels. He's by the fire

later, listening back to the great day,
though to the untrained ear there's nothing much
doing: a booming breeze, a wasp or bee
trying its empty button-hole, a stitch

of wrensong now and then. But he listens late
and nods off to the creak of the spinal pole
and the rumble of his tractor pulling beets
in the bottom field, which cuts out. In a while

somebody will approach over ploughed earth
in caked Frankenstein boots. There'll be a noise
of tearing, and he'll flap awake by a hearth
grown cold, waking the house with broken cries.

An Orrery of Hats

Everything in this display is moving
  and circling nearest to its sun are snoods
only meant to last a shift – they take
  hours to orbit. The party crowns
which see the light of day just once a year
  are meteoric, but if we stand well back
there's outer planets in the wings, top hats
  moving into a comet's night – we'll not
be seeing much more of them in our lifetimes
  though their sheen will come around again to grace
the evenings – and bonnets of beaverskin
  have reached the boreal brim; a naval rating's
peaked affair still has the salt-stained band
  from the night the ship went down with all hands,
sinking to the bottom of the clock;
  and look how many feathered confections float
as satellites that send no signal back,
  an entire species lost to a brief craze.
Passing through a belt of baseball caps, it's good
  to think of all the checks and tweeds sent up
as objects in a deep-space probe, and hope
  that, on a night no one will live to see,
a deerstalker on its lonely course
  could provide the only clue to who we were
in some far corner of the universe.

The Anecdote

i.m.

The seating plan: I'm led to my table
near the exits with the other untelevisables
and the wheelchair-bound, nervous because they've sat me
opposite one of my heroes, Eduardo Paolozzi,

whose *Recurring Themes* I was given the night before
I left home for good. A morning in September
1985, the bed-sheets soaked
as if the ghost of my childhood had upped sticks,

and later, the big Paolozzi outside Euston,
a graphite berg fetched up in Zone 1 London.
I spent those first months in Paolozziville –
machine-head men; splintered mosaic tiles

on the Underground – and saw him the following summer
rooting through the bargain box in Zwemmer's:
bull-like, gigantic hands, riffling, weighing-up
the colour plates, telling the whole shop

how he was going to rip and cut and paste.
There was even a story of Picasso as a collagist
and I imagine this could break the ice:
So did the two of you come face to face?

When I took my seat he didn't take my hand.
Something had struck him down. He couldn't stand
for the toast, or speak a word. I think you're meant
to report back from such eyes a spark or glint

of recognition beyond motor effects
but if I'm honest there was nothing, except
the flash of forks, the wink of cutlery,
and a tiny, fish-eyed reflection of me.

Paperboy and Air Rifle

A little hunter, I could have shouldered a gun
in the Highlands or Apennines. I would have loved
a wax jacket with a poacher's pocket sewn in,
but at Gerrard's Lane, where I reached the furthest point

and letterbox from the newsagent, where the fields
began, I took wood micks, shebbies, spadgers;
would have taken game if there'd been any to take;
would have knocked a partridge from the head of her brood,

I was that mean. I was doing all right at school,
shining in English composition, my similes
like my reading age running on ahead of the class:
The instant noodles hang from the end of my fork

like a Portuguese man-o-war. But I lived for the light nights
walking home on my own, all the papers delivered, a bird
in the bag. I've never been happier than the time
I got a goldfinch, looked it over in my hand –

just a line of blood between the mandibles –
and, taking the shortcut through a thistle field,
a summer's worth of goldfinches, the rest of his charm,
flew with me, a little ahead of me, from crown to crown.

The Westbourne at Sloane Square

You again! Of all the bomb-scarred stonework
and air vents underfoot I knew by heart.
You, still going strong in your black pipe
above the passengers and mice-live tracks.
You, flowing through eighteenth-century parkscape
into an ironclad late-Victorian night.

Pissed and standing on the eastbound platform
I was a tin soldier who'd fallen in
to London's storm drain, sent spinning around
the Circle Line long after closing time,
and all along I've carried these trapped sounds
I hear again and recognise deep down.

How many miles of shit have you crawled through
since we last met? I'd do it all again.
We've less choice than we think, the likes of you and me.
Blind water, borne along or bearing through,
escaping in a hurry for open sea.
To think we start as innocent as rain.

Landy

Ellen MacArthur coins this word from the deck
of her trimaran, sniffing the air for England.
She's just sailed round the world and so the scent
is truffles mixed with bonfires and earth.

Before the lit flares and the horns of the harbour,
before sat-cam gives way to rolling news,
Ellen crosses the finish line alone.
Landfall comes with an armada's view.

She's looked into the mediaeval night,
into a high cathedral dome of stars
so clear – so far from any other source of light –
it seemed a stellar ladder could reach them all:

Betelgeuse's glowing coal, the Pleiades'
smelt works at full stretch, galactic smoke
bellowed through dark woods. The world was made
then melted down. The sea has seen it all

but solo yachtswomen can glimpse the whole
dark night suspended in a greater dark.
Those tears caught live, that farewell to her craft,
could be relief and flash photography,

but Ellen MacArthur could just as easily
weep comet meltwater and cosmic dust
for all she used to understand as home.
Stepping ashore, the ground might scorch her feet.

Dormouse Stronghold

Over a hundred years we've fortified
our range; at the last count just thirty miles
from where we escaped The Collections: while the mink
and grey squirrel are coming soon to a place
near you (if they're not there already) you'll find
us keeping ourselves to ourselves, only breeding if
the beech harvest is good, sleeping the northern
winters off, bingeing through good autumns.

Think of me as everymouse, whom the Romans ate
and the raindrop coshed, as I climbed and sprung the stalk
in fields where ploughs turn up pieces of pot;
Rome fell, but here my radius reaches out
to Luton, Leighton Buzzard, the green on the map,
the blur in the wing mirror, the hills from a train;
a conquest of the back gardens slow as money
taking root, as it does. I've noticed of late

the arrival of the dormouse box, and I'll take
to this like a stockade. So civilised.
Crawling out under a sky brilliant with stars
a few degrees out of whack, full of dead gods
and symbols I'll outlive, I feel a rush
pass through me, tip to tail, like the express
heading north, for what lies ahead, for whatever's past.
Before the night's hard work, I allow myself that.

I Ran All the Way Home

after Joe Brainard

I remember waking up around the time of the moon landings and flicking a single Sugar Puff from my pillow, and then turning over to find hundreds more where I'd been sick in the night.

I remember being scared of bottle rockets and having my hair washed.

I remember being scared of the credits to *The Champions*.

I remember we would wake our dad in the night if we wanted to pee, and he would perch us on the rim of the bath to do it.

I remember being told a flowerbed in the Botanic Gardens had once been a pond, but they'd filled it in, and this being the most mysterious thing in my life for a long time.

I remember dark green seawater sloshing against Roman numerals and dock steps.

I remember the smell of the underground railway.

I remember it teeming down for days.

I remember my uncle who'd been in the navy showing me paperbacks with semi-naked women on the covers, and telling me Kiev in Russia was the worst place he'd ever been.

I remember walking out of shops without my change.

I remember checking mousetraps with a big square torch.

I remember one kid called Philip who threw up watery streams everywhere on the first day of school. I don't remember ever seeing him again.

I remember the 'show house'.

I remember having to wear the woolly boots: these were a pair of pink knitted bootees that hung on ribbons next to Miss Jump's blackboard, and any boy caught kung-fu kicking or raising his feet had to put them on for a day.

I remember graffiti: KILLER CELTIC on a wall in Netherley, TAXI WHORE on the footbridge at Belle Vale Shopping Precinct, LES GROOVES DOGS BOTTIES on the railway at Childwall.

I remember *Liverpool: City of Change and Challenge*.

I remember lime-green sleep in my eyes.

I remember learning to play rounders and my friend Valentine was the back-stop, and after striking the ball I threw the bat into his face three times, and I remember his astonishment.

I remember one of our neighbours, a mechanic, walking past our house one night covered in oil. I said 'All right' but he just ignored me, and the next day I learned that he'd been beaten with a tyre-iron and that blood looks black under streetlight.

I remember 'The Bump'.

I remember you had to either rub cayenne pepper onto your cock, or take a branding from a pair of metal compasses heated in the gas ring, if you wanted to be in our gang.

I remember one gang punishment was being rubbed all over with Tiger Balm.

I remember fully carpeted backfield dens.

I remember making 'birds' nests' out of cut grass.

I remember acorns.

I remember 'driving' in burned-out cars.

I remember running up the ramp of the apron at The Abbey and touching the screen, expecting it to be warm, but it was cold.

I remember walking for miles on hot days, down long

straight industrial roads out towards the chemical works at Widnes.

I remember meeting tramps in the road.

I remember keeping watch inside the unlit bonfire. Rival streets would come to steal prime firewood in the night.
I remember there being an actual door opening onto a hollow.

I remember learning to smoke and liking the older brands like Senior Service and Player's because I imagined they connected me with a maritime world that had vanished, even though Consulate and More had the better taste.

I remember going to see 'the Lights'.

I remember how crabs never survived the journey home in a carrier bag.

I remember if you put your hand in a bird's nest to check for eggs you had to blow on it afterwards to remove your scent. Otherwise the bird would abandon the nest.

I remember the sound in my head after being punched for the first time was like the test-card tone.

I remember kaolin and morphine separated in a bottle under the sink.

I remember the medicine cabinet and the meter cupboard and the bin shed and the airing cupboard.

I remember stories of kids falling into the tanks at the sewage works, and how there was never anything left of them but an eyeball, or a toe.

I remember *If I should die before I wake/I pray the Lord my soul to take*.

I remember Marco Polo and Bully Forbes and the Black Ball Line.

I remember we lived by the bus terminus, and drivers would send us in for chips or cigarettes, and some girls hung around waiting to be let on at the stand, the doors hissing shut behind them.

I remember being honoured to fetch Chopper his curry, rice and chips.

I remember going for brawn, and the sign in Ernie the Butcher's: *A missing knife is a danger to all*.

I remember a lad held a knife to my throat on the 73 for a laugh.

I remember one night in bed realising I was definitely going to die and wondering what nothing would feel like. This was around the same time as realising the universe went on forever.

I remember breaking my arm and getting the bus into town to hospital. After the arm was set, my dad stopped off at a pub. I waited in the doorway, and he came out with lemonade and crisps. It was a struggle to eat crisps with my arm up in a sling.

I remember watching the flats being knocked down, enjoying the thud of the wrecking ball against wallpapered rooms open to the air, and thinking about how flimsy our homes really were.

I remember Saturday teatimes were egg and chips with 'Sports Report' and the pools coupons.

I remember Sunday teatimes were Spam and tongue and salad, and ice cream with hundreds-and-thousands.

I remember 'his eyes are bigger than his belly'.

I remember Sundays in the deserted city centre; Williamson Square in the rain.

I remember the smell of cabbage and a programme called *Out of Town*.

I remember a girl called Denise Custard who could tap dance.

I remember Miss Clarkson danced a 'slowie' with me on the last night of a trip to North Wales.

I remember some dogs had the run of their streets.

I remember King, a German shepherd, who had a crumbling spine; Buster, a kind of grey electrified mop head; Bruce, a black Lab, who had a patch of mange in the middle of his back; Sandor, a giant (I think) Newfoundland, who arrived out of nowhere and caused chaos for a few days every summer.

I remember my sister and me called 'Do You Know the Way to San Jose?' the 'Doggie Song' when it came on the radio because the backing vocals sounded like barking, to us.

I remember *A porky prime cut* ...

I remember being told the devil lived in the hot valves at the back of the television. I can't remember who told me this.

I remember my first night in London. It was a shared room in a hostel in Knightsbridge, and somebody had carved *I stumbled into town* into the headboard.